ACHARI PANEER TIKAS

MAKHMALI PANEER

GW00420609

MALPAUS WITH SHAHI RABADI

tarladalal.com
● THE LARGEST INDIAN FOOD SITE ●

OVER 1,80,000 REGISTERED MEMBERS

*B*ECOME A GOLD

OR SILVER MEMBER

ON TARLADALAL.COM

AND FIND ALL YOUR

FAVOURITE RECIPES.

For further information mail us at
subscription@tarladalal.com
or call on our helpline no. 022-2496 8068
on all weekdays between
9.30 am and 4.30 pm.

PHOTOGRAPH BY JIGNESH JHAVERI

Paneer

Tarla Dalal
India's #1 Cookery Author

S&C

SANJAY & CO.
MUMBAI

Fourth Printing : 2005

Copyright © Sanjay & Co.

ISBN : 81-86469-90-7

All rights reserved with the publishers.

No part of this book may be reproduced, stored in a retrieval system or transmitted by any means, electronic, mechanical, photocopying, recording or otherwise, without the written permission of the publishers.

Price: Rs.89/-

Published & Distributed by : **Sanjay & Company**

353/A-1, Shah & Nahar Industrial Estate, Dhanraj Mill Compound,
Lower Parel (W), Mumbai - 400 013. INDIA.
Tel. : (91-22) 2496 8068 • Fax : (91-22) 2496 5876 • E-mail : sanjay@tarladalal.com

Printed by : **Jupiter Prints**, Mumbai

Recipe Research & Production Design	**Nutritionist**	**Photography**	**Design**
Pinky Chandan Dixit	Nisha Katira	Jignesh Jhaveri	Satyamangal Rege
Arati Fedane	**Food Stylist**	**Typesetting**	
Pradnya Sundararaj	Shubhangi Dhaimade	Adityas Enterprises	

DISCLAMIER

While every precaution has been taken in the preparation of this book, the publishers and the author assume no responsibility for errors or omissions. Neither is any liability assumed for damages resulting from the use of information contained herein. And of course, no book is a substitute for a qualified medical advice. So it is wiser to modify your dietary patterns under the supervision of a doctor or a nutritionist.

BULK PURCHASES

Tarla Dalal Cookbooks are ideal gifts. If you are interested in buying more than 500 assorted copies of Tarla Dalal Cookbooks at special prices, please contact us at 91-22-2496 8068 or email : sanjay@tarladalal.com

— INTRODUCTION —

Prepared traditionally from buffalo milk, paneer is a completely vegetarian cheese. A staple ingredient in many Indian dishes, it has been extracted since ancient times from surplus milk thereby preventing spoilage in our warm Asian climate. Served fresh or deep fried, it tastes delicious in subzis, snacks and sweets.

Abounding with protein and calcium, paneer is one of two most important nutrients in a vegetarian diet. Every 100g of paneer contains 292 calories, 13.4 gm of protein and above all muscle strengthening 480 mg of calcium.

Paneer is one of my favourite foods. I enjoyed putting this book together...Paneer Butter Masala, Lifafa Parathas, Crispy Cottage Cheese Tortillas, Pahadi Tikkas are just a few of the recipes featured inside.

So enter the world of **PANEER**. Turn the pages and enthrall yourself with the many wonderful ways in which you can use this versatile ingredient.

Happy Cooking !

~ HANDY HINTS FOR USING PANEER ~

➤ Paneer has a high moisture content and so must be refrigerated as it has a short shelf – life. Store the block of paneer in a bowl filled with cold water. Change the water everyday.

➤ When stored for long, paneer becomes hard and crumbly especially if you're using frozen paneer. To soften it again, just dunk it in hot water for a few minutes and then drain out all the water.

➤ While deep frying paneer fry it quickly over a high flame and drain on absorbent paper. If you like you can store it in a bowl of warm water to keep it moist. Add it to the gravy just before you wish to serve it.

➤ If the paneer is dry and crumbly, use it to make koftas or a burjee it's the best way to rescue it.

➤ Paneer can absorb other flavours, and so is excellent for marinating and grilling.

~ CONTENTS ~

SUBZIS

SNACKS

BASIC RECIPE

Subzis

BABYCORN AUR PANEER KA SALAN

Picture on cover

🍂 Preparation time : 15 minutes.   🍂 Cooking time : 45 minutes.   🍂 Serves 4.

1 cup babycorn, cut into 25 mm. (1") pieces
½ cup paneer (cottage cheese), cut into 12 mm. (½") cubes
2 Bhavnagri chillies, thickly sliced
2 cups onions, finely chopped
2 tbsp roasted peanuts
2 tbsp sesame seeds (til)
2 tbsp desiccated coconut
1 tsp fennel seeds (saunf)
1 tsp onion seeds (kalonji)
2 tsp ginger-green chilli paste
1 tsp garlic paste
½ tsp chilli powder
1 tsp coriander (dhania) powder
¼ tsp turmeric powder (haldi)
1 cup tomatoes, finely chopped

1 tsp tamarind (imli), soaked in ¼ cup of water
2 tsp grated jaggery (gur)
4 tbsp oil
salt to taste

Other ingredients
oil for deep frying

1. Boil the babycorn in water till it is cooked. Drain and keep aside.
2. Deep fry the Bhavnagri chillies in hot oil for a few seconds. Remove, drain on absorbent paper and keep aside.
3. Heat the oil in a pan, add the onions and sauté till they turn golden brown in colour.
4. Add the peanuts, sesame seeds, desiccated coconut, fennel seeds, onion seeds, ginger-green chilli paste, garlic paste and sauté over a slow flame till all the ingredients are browned.
5. Add the chilli powder, coriander powder, turmeric powder, tomatoes and salt and cook till the tomatoes soften. Cool completely.
6. Grind the gravy to a smooth paste in a blender, using a little water if required.

7. Combine the gravy with tamarind pulp, 1 cup of water and jaggery in a pan, bring to a boil and simmer till the oil separates. Add the Bhavnagri chillies, babycorn and paneer and mix well.
Serve hot.

Handy tip : The salan has to be cooked for a long time to get the actual authentic flavour and colour of the gravy.

PANEER KALIMIRCH

2 cups paneer (cottage cheese), cut into 12 mm. (½") cubes
¼ cup fresh cream
2 tbsp milk
¼ tsp turmeric powder (haldi)
¼ tsp garam masala
1 tsp freshly crushed peppercons
2 tbsp oil
salt to taste

To be ground into a smooth paste
1½ cups onion, chopped
½ cup cashewnuts
4 cloves garlic
6 mm. (¼") piece ginger

1. Heat the oil in a pan and fry the paste for 4 to 5 minutes while stirring
   continuously.

2. Add the paneer, cream, milk, turmeric powder, salt and 2 tbsp of water and cook for a few minutes.
3. Add the garam masala and crushed peppercorns. Mix well.
Serve hot.

PANEER PASANDA

◆ Preparation time : 20 minutes.   ◆ Cooking time : 20 minutes.   ◆ Serves 4.

1½ cups paneer (cottage cheese), cut into 12 mm. (½") cubes

For the onion and cashew paste
1 cup onions, roughly chopped
5 cloves garlic
12 mm. (½") piece ginger
2 tbsp cashewnuts, broken

For the brown onion paste
2 onions, sliced
oil for deep frying

Other ingredients
1 tsp chilli powder
½ tsp garam masala
1 cup curds, whisked
2 tbsp oil

salt to taste

For the garnish
2 tsp fresh cream

For the onion and cashew paste
1. Boil the onions in 1 cup of water until soft.
2. Add the garlic, ginger and cashewnuts and grind into a smooth paste.

For the brown onion paste
1. Deep fry the onions in oil until golden brown. Remove and drain on absorbent paper.
2. Grind into a smooth paste in a blender using a little water.

How to proceed
1. Heat the oil in a pan. Add the onion and cashew paste and cook over a slow flame for a few minutes.
2. Add the chilli powder and garam masala, mix and cook again till the mixture leaves oil.
3. Take the pan off the fire, add the curds and mix well.
4. Simmer for 5 to 6 minutes, while stirring continuously.
5. Add the brown onion paste and salt and simmer for another 2 minutes.
6. Add the paneer, garnish with the cream and serve hot.

QUICK CORN AND PANEER SUBZI

* Preparation time : 10 minutes.   * Cooking time : 10 minutes.   * Serves 4.

1 cup sweet corn kernels (makai ka dana)
1 cup paneer (cottage cheese), cut into 12 mm. (½") cubes
1 cup onions, sliced
½ cup capsicum, sliced
1 cup tomatoes, sliced
1 tsp roasted cumin (jeera) powder
½ tsp chilli powder
2 tbsp oil
salt to taste

1. Heat the oil in a pan and fry the onions. Add the sweet corn and capsicum and cook for at least 3 to 4 minutes.
2. Add the tomatoes and fry again.
3. Add the cumin powder, chilli powder and salt. Mix well and cook for 1 minute.
4. Add the paneer and cook for 3 to 4 minutes. Serve hot.

Handy tip : Parboil the corn kernels they are is not tender.

QUICK PANEER AND VEGETABLE KORMA

Picture on facing page

❧ Preparation time : 10 minutes.   ❧ Cooking time : 20 minutes.   ❧ Serves 4.

½ cup paneer (cottage cheese), cut into 12 mm. (½") cubes
¼ cup cauliflower, cut into small florets
¼ cup French beans, cut into 12 mm. (½") cubes
¼ cup carrots, cut into 12 mm. (½") cubes
¼ cup green peas
½ cup capsicum, cut into 12 mm. (½") cubes
¼ cup babycorn, cut into slices
1 cup onions, puréed
½ tsp cumin seeds (jeera)
2 cloves (laung)
1 stick cinnamon (dalchini)
1 green cardamom (elaichi)
1 tsp ginger-garlic paste
½ tsp green chilli paste
1 cup milk

Quick Paneer and Vegetable Korma : Recipe above →

¼ cup canned pineapple slices, cut into small pieces
3 tbsp fresh cream
½ tsp garam masala
1 tbsp oil
salt to taste

For the garnish
canned pineapple slices
chopped coriander

1. Heat the oil in a pan and add the cumin seeds. When the seeds crackle, add the onion purée, cloves, cinnamon, cardamom, ginger-garlic paste, green chilli paste and sauté for 5 to 7 minutes while stirring continuously.
2. Add the cauliflower, French beans, carrot, green peas, capsicum, babycorn, salt, ½ cup of milk and ¼ cup of water. Cover and cook over a slow flame till the vegetables are tender.
3. Add the remaining milk, paneer, pineapple, cream and garam masala and cook for another 3 to 4 minutes.
   Garnish with pineapple slices and chopped coriander and serve hot.

PANEER PALAK

2 cups paneer (cottage cheese), cut into 12 mm. (½") cubes
10 cups spinach (palak) leaves
¾ cup onion, finely chopped
4 cloves garlic
12 mm. (½") piece ginger, grated
2 green chillies, finely chopped
½ tsp turmeric powder (haldi)
¾ cup tomato purée, page 102
¼ tsp garam masala
2 tbsp oil
salt to taste

Other ingredients
oil for deep frying

1. Blanch the spinach in a big vessel of boiling water.
2. Drain, wash with cold water and blend in a liquidiser to a smooth purée.
3. Cut the paneer into small pieces and deep fry in hot oil until golden brown.
4. Remove and drain on absorbent paper. Keep aside.
5. Heat the oil in a pan and fry the onions till they turn translucent.
6. Add the garlic, ginger, green chillies and turmeric powder and fry again for a little time.
7. Add the tomato purée and fry stirring continuously till the mixture leaves oil.
8. Add the spinach purée, paneer, garam masala, and salt 1 cup of water and bring to boil.
   Serve hot.

DAHIWALI PANEER SUBZI

❧ Preparation time : 6 minutes.   ❧ Cooking time : 7 minutes.   ❧ Serves 2.

1 cup paneer (cottage cheese), cut into 12 mm. (½") cubes
1 tsp fennel seeds (saunf)
¼ tsp mustard seeds (rai)
5 to 6 fenugreek (methi) seeds
1 tsp onions seeds (kalonji)
½ tsp cumin seeds (jeera)
½ tsp asafoetida (hing)
½ cup onion, sliced
½ tsp turmeric powder (haldi)
½ tsp chilli powder
½ tsp black salt (sanchal)
¾ cup fresh curds
1 tsp plain flour (maida)
3 tbsp chopped coriander
1 tbsp oil
salt to taste

1. Mix the fennel seeds, mustard seeds, fenugreek seeds, onion seeds, cumin seeds and asafoetida in a small bowl.
2. Heat the oil in a pan and add the seed mixture.
3. When they crackle, add the onions and sauté till they turn translucent.
4. Add the paneer, turmeric powder, chilli powder, black salt and stir for some time.
5. Whisk together and add the curds and plain flour. Mix well.
6. Add the coriander and salt and bring to a boil.
   Serve hot with rice or rotis.

BABYCORN PANEER JALFRAZIE

❧ Preparation time : 10 minutes.   ❧ Cooking time : 15 minutes.   ❧ Serves 4.

12 nos. babycorn, cut into 4 lengthwise
1¼ cups paneer (cottage cheese), cut into 25 mm. (1") strips
¼ tsp cumin seeds (jeera)
⅛ tsp asafoetida (hing)
1 tsp ginger-green chilli paste
¾ cup spring onions whites, sliced
¾ cup spring onions greens, chopped
¾ cup capsicum, sliced
¼ tsp turmeric powder (haldi)
½ tsp chilli powder
½ cup tomato purée, page 102
2 tbsp chopped coriander
1 tbsp oil
salt to taste

1. Heat the oil in a pan and add the cumin seeds and asafoetida. When they crackle, add the ginger-green chilli paste, spring onion whites and capsicum and sauté for 2 minutes.
2. Add the babycorn, turmeric powder, chilli powder, tomato purée and salt and sauté on a slow flame for 4 to 5 minutes till the babycorn is cooked.
3. Add the paneer and spring onion greens and toss lightly.
   Garnish with the chopped coriander and serve hot.

BROCCOLI ALOO AUR PANEER KI SUBZI

❧ Preparation time : 10 minutes.   ❧ Cooking time : 15 minutes.   ❧ Serves 4.

1 cup broccoli florets
1 cup potato, cut into 12 mm. (½") cubes
½ cup paneer (cottage cheese), cut into 12 mm. (½") cubes
½ cup peeled white baby onions
1 tsp ginger-garlic paste
1 tsp chilli flakes (paprika)
1 tsp oil
salt to taste

1. Heat the oil in a pan, add the ginger-garlic paste and baby onions and sauté for a few minutes.
2. Add the potatoes and salt and sauté for another 4 to 5 minutes.
3. Add 2 to 3 tbsp of water and broccoli and cook till the potatoes are done.
4. Add the paneer and chilli flakes, mix well and sauté for 4 to 5 minutes.
   Serve hot.

PANEER CAPSICUM STIR-FRY

❧ Preparation time : 30 minutes.   ❧ Cooking time : 20 minutes.   ❧ Serves 4.

2 cups paneer (cottage cheese), cut into thin long strips
½ cup capsicum, cut into thin strips
1 tsp coriander (dhania) seeds
1 whole dry red chilli
2 green chillies, finely chopped
½ tsp chopped ginger
¾ cup tomatoes, chopped
¼ tsp kasuri methi (dry fenugreek leaves)
1 tbsp chopped coriander
1 tbsp oil
salt to taste

To be ground to a smooth paste
6 cloves garlic, mixed with a little water

1. Pound the coriander seeds and red chilli together. Keep aside.

2. Heat the oil in a pan, add the garlic paste and cook on a slow flame for a few seconds.
3. Add the capsicum and pounded spices and cook on a slow flame for 30 seconds.
4. Add the green chillies and ginger and fry again for a few seconds.
5. Add the tomatoes and cook until the mixture leaves oil.
6. Add the kasuri methi and salt and fry again for a few seconds.
7. Finally, add the sliced paneer and cook for a few minutes.
   Garnish with the coriander and serve hot.

PANEER IN QUICK WHITE GRAVY

❧ Preparation time : 10 minutes. ❧ Cooking time : 10 minutes. ❧ Serves 4.

2 cups paneer (cottage cheese), cut into 12 mm. (½") cubes
¼ tsp garam masala
3 tbsp fresh cream
2 tbsp milk
2 tbsp oil

To be ground into a paste
1 cup onions, chopped
1 tbsp cashewnuts
4 cloves garlic
6 mm. (¼") piece ginger

1. Heat the oil in a pan and fry the paste. Add the garam masala and fry again.
2. Add the paneer, cream, milk and 2 tbsp of water and cook for a few minutes.
   Serve hot.

PANEER KOFTAS IN SPINACH SAUCE

❦ Preparation time : 15 minutes.   ❦ Cooking time : 30 minutes.   ❦ Serves 6.

For the spinach sauce
2 cups spinach (palak), finely chopped
½ cup fresh curds
½ tsp sugar
2 tbsp oil
salt to taste

To be ground into a paste (for the spinach sauce)
1 tbsp grated fresh coconut
1 tbsp chopped cashewnuts
1 tbsp poppy seeds (khus-khus)
4 cloves garlic
4 to 5 green chillies
25 mm. (1") piece ginger
1 tsp fennel seeds (saunf)

For the koftas

1½ cups paneer (cottage cheese), grated
4 tbsp plain flour (maida)
2 tbsp chopped coriander
2 green chillies, finely chopped
a pinch soda bi-carb
salt to taste

Other ingredients

oil for deep frying

For the spinach sauce

1. Whisk the curds till smooth. Keep aside.
2. Cook the spinach with ½ cup of water.
3. When cooked, drain and blend in a liquidiser till smooth.
4. Heat the oil in a pan, and fry the paste for 3 to 4 minutes.
5. Add the curds and fry again for 1 minute.
6. Add the spinach purée, sugar and salt and boil for 3 to 4 minutes.

For the koftas

1. Mix all the ingredients and shape into small balls.

2. Deep fry in hot oil until golden brown.
3. Remove, drain on absorbent paper and keep aside.

How to proceed
Just before serving, add the koftas to the spinach sauce and bring to boil.
Serve hot.

PANEER MASALA

❬ Preparation time : 30 minutes.   ❬ Cooking time : 20 minutes.   ❬ Serves 4.

2 cups paneer (cottage cheese)
¾ cup tomatoes, chopped
½ cup fresh cream
1 tsp chilli sauce (optional)
3 tbsp oil
oil for deep frying
salt to taste

To be ground into a paste
¾ cup onions, chopped
1 tbsp poppy seeds (khus-khus)
1 tbsp grated fresh coconut
2 sticks cinnamon (dalchini)
2 cloves (laung)
10 peppercorns
6 whole dry red Kashmiri chillies
3 tsp coriander (dhania) seeds

1½ tsp cumin seeds (jeera)
5 cloves garlic
25 mm. (1") piece ginger

1. Cut the paneer into long pieces and deep fry in hot oil. Remove, drain on absorbent paper and keep aside.
2. Heat the oil in a pan and fry the paste for at least 3 to 4 minutes.
3. Add the chopped tomatoes and fry again for 3 to 4 minutes.
4. Add the paneer pieces, cream, chilli sauce, salt and 1 cup of water and cook for 10 minutes.

Serve hot with parathas.

PANEER BUTTER MASALA

❧ Preparation time : 15 minutes.   ❧ Cooking time : 20 minutes.   ❧ Serves 4.

3 cups paneer (cottage cheese), cut into long strips
1 tsp kasuri methi (dried fenugreek leaves)
¼ cup onions, chopped
2 tbsp butter

To be ground into a paste
1 cup onions, chopped
25 mm. (1") piece ginger
6 to 7 cloves garlic
2 tbsp broken cashewnuts

Other ingredients
1 tsp chilli powder
2 cups fresh tomato purée, page 102
1 tsp cumin (jeera) powder
½ tsp garam masala

Mutter Paneer Butter Masala : Recipe on page 38 →

1 tbsp honey
¼ cup milk
¼ cup fresh cream
1 tbsp oil
salt to taste

1. Heat the oil in a pan, add the ground paste and cook till it is light brown in colour.
2. Add the chilli powder and tomato purée and cook for a few minutes.
3. Add the cumin powder, garam masala and ½ cup of water and cook for some time till the oil separates from the masala. Keep aside.
4. In another pan, melt the butter, add the kasuri methi and onions and cook till the onions are lightly browned.
5. Add this to the tomato gravy, along with the honey, milk, cream, paneer and salt and allow it to come to a boil.
   Serve hot with rotis or parathas.

VARIATION : MUTTER PANEER BUTTER MASALA Picture on page 37
You can add ½ cup boiled peas at step 5 and bring the curry to a boil.

PANEER KORMA

Preparation time : 10 minutes.   Cooking time : 20 minutes.   Serves 4.

2 cups paneer (cottage cheese), cut into 12 mm. (½") cubes
2 medium sized tomatoes
¾ cup onions, grated
1 tsp chilli powder
½ cup fresh cream
¼ tsp turmeric powder (haldi)
2 green cardamoms (elaichi)
2 tbsp chopped coriander
3 tbsp oil
salt to taste

1. Put the tomatoes in hot water. After 10 minutes remove, take off the skin and chop.
2. Heat the oil in a pan, fry the onions and cardamoms till they turn translucent.
3. Add the tomatoes and cook till the mixture leaves oil.
4. Add the chilli powder and turmeric powder and fry for a few minutes.
5. Add the paneer, cream and salt.
   Garnish with the coriander and serve hot.

PANEER KHURCHAN

✦ Preparation time : 10 minutes.   ✦ Cooking time : 10 minutes.   ✦ Serves 4.

2 cups paneer (cottage cheese), cut into 5 mm. (¼") cubes
2 tomatoes, finely chopped
½ tsp cumin seeds (jeera)
½ cup onions, finely chopped
¼ tsp turmeric powder (haldi)
¼ tsp chilli powder
a few drops lemon juice (optional)
3 tbsp oil
salt to taste

For the garnish
1 green chilli, finely chopped
2 tbsp chopped coriander

1. Heat the oil in a pan on a high flame. Add the cumin seeds and fry for a few seconds. When they crackle, add the onions and fry again till they turn golden brown.

2. Add the paneer and tomatoes and cook for 2 minutes. While cooking, add the turmeric powder, chilli powder and salt. If the paneer sticks to the bottom, scrape with a spatula. Repeat again every time it sticks to the bottom until the paneer gets soft.
3. Scrape the paneer from the pan into a bowl and garnish with the green chilli and coriander.
   Serve hot.

Handy tip : The trick is to let the paneer and masala stick for a few seconds each time before stirring it on the pan. This gives it both its name and flavour.

PANEER-BHUTTA SUBZI

❧ Preparation time : 10 minutes.   ❧ Cooking time : 10 minutes.   ❧ Serves 4.

2 cups paneer (cottage cheese), cut into 12 mm. (½") cubes
2 cups sweet corn kernels (makai ka dana)
½ tsp cumin seeds (jeera)
½ cup onions, chopped
2 green chillies, chopped finely
¼ tsp turmeric powder (haldi)
½ tsp sugar
½ tsp garam masala
2 tbsp chopped coriander
2 tbsp oil
salt to taste

1. Heat the oil in a pan and add the cumin seeds.
2. When the cumin seeds crackle, add the onions and green chillies and sauté for some time.
3. Add the sweet corn kernels, paneer, turmeric, sugar, salt and some water.
4. Heat till the sweet corn kernels get cooked and then add the garam masala and coriander. Toss well and serve hot.

PANEER METHI CHAMAN

1 cup paneer (cottage cheese), cut into 25 mm. (1") cubes
2 cups fenugreek (methi) leaves, chopped
4 cups spinach (palak), chopped
a pinch soda bi-carb
1 tsp cumin seeds (jeera)
¼ cup onions, chopped
¼ tsp asafoetida (hing)
a pinch turmeric powder (haldi)
¼ tsp red chilli powder
¼ tsp coriander (dhania) powder
1 tsp ginger-green chilli paste
1 tsp kasuri methi (dried fenugreek leaves)
¼ tsp garam masala
2 tbsp oil
salt to taste

1. Roast the kasuri methi in a pan till crisp. Keep aside.
2. Boil the spinach and fenugreek leaves in ¼ cup of water with a pinch of soda bi-carb until soft. Blend in a blender and keep aside.
3. Heat oil in a pan. Add the cumin seeds and onions and sauté for 1 minute.
4. Add the asafoetida, turmeric powder, red chilli powder, coriander powder, ginger-green chilli paste and kasuri methi and fry again.
5. Add the blended mixture, paneer, garam masala and ½ cup water and bring to a boil.
   Serve hot.

NAVARATNA CURRY

∾ Preparation time : 25 minutes.   ∾ Cooking time : 40 minutes.   ∾ Serves 4.

½ cup paneer (cottage cheese), cut into 12 mm. (½" cubes)
½ cup French beans, cut into 12 mm. (½") pieces
½ cup carrots, cut into 12 mm. (½") cubes
½ cup potatoes, cut into 12 mm. (½") cubes
½ cup cauliflower florets
½ cup capsicum, cut into 12 mm. (½") cubes
½ cup broken cashewnuts
2 tbsp raisins
¾ cup green peas, boiled
¼ cup tomato purée, page 102
½ cup curds
2 tbsp oil
salt to taste
sugar to taste

To be ground into a paste
3 cloves garlic
½ green chilli
2 whole dry red kashmiri chillies
12 mm. (½") piece ginger
½ tsp coriander (dhania) seeds
½ tsp cumin seeds (jeera)
½ tsp shahjeera (caraway seeds)
1 green cardamom (elaichi)

For the garnish
1 sheet edible silver leaf (varq)
¼ cup pineapple pieces
2 to 3 cherries

Other ingredients
oil for deep frying

1. Boil the French beans, carrots, cauliflower and green peas. Drain and keep aside.
2. Deep fry the potatoes and paneer separately in hot oil till done. Remove, drain on absorbent paper and keep aside.

3. Whisk the curds till smooth. Keep aside.
4. Heat oil in a pan and fry the ground paste for 2 to 3 minutes.
5. Add the tomato purée and curds and fry again stirring continuously till the mixture leaves oil.
6. Add the capsicum and sauté for 1 to 2 minutes.
7. Add boiled vegetables, potatoes, paneer, cashewnuts, raisins, peas, salt, sugar and ½ cup of water and cook for a few minutes to bring to a boil.

    Serve hot garnished with the silver leaf, pineapple pieces and cherries.

PANEER MAKAI

❧ Preparation time : 10 minutes.   ❧ Cooking time : 20 minutes.   ❧ Serves 4.

1½ cups paneer (cottage cheese), cut into 12 mm. (½") cubes
1 cup sweet corn kernels (makai ka dana)
3 capsicums, thinly sliced
1 tsp cumin seeds (jeera)
¼ tsp asafoetida (hing)
1 tsp chopped green chillies
1½ tsp grated ginger
a pinch sugar
3 tbsp chopped coriander
3 tbsp oil
salt to taste

1. Purée the sweet corn kernels with ½ cup of water to a fine paste in a blender and keep aside.
2. Heat 2 tbsp of oil in a pan and sauté the capsicums and paneer till they are lightly browned. Remove and keep aside.

3. Heat the remaining 1 tbsp of oil in the same pan and add the cumin seeds and asafoetida.
4. When the cumin seeds crackle, add the green chillies and ginger, sauté for a few seconds and add the puréed corn.
5. Add 1½ cups of water, sugar and salt and bring it to a boil.
6. Add the sautéed capsicum and paneer and coriander and mix well.
Serve hot with parathas of your choice.

URAD DAL WITH PANEER

☙ Preparation time : 20 minutes.   ☙ Cooking time : 30 minutes.   ☙ Serves 4.

1 cup paneer (cottage cheese), cut into 12 mm. (½") cubes
1 cup urad dal (split black lentil), soaked for one hour
½ cup onions, chopped
½ tsp shahjeera (caraway seeds)
½ cup tomato, chopped
2 green chillies, finely chopped
½ tsp chilli powder
¼ tsp turmeric powder
2 tbsp chopped coriander
3 tbsp oil
salt to taste

1. Heat water with the turmeric powder and salt and when it comes to a boil, add the urad dal and cook till it becomes tender. Strain to remove excess water. Keep aside.
2. Heat the oil on a tava (griddle) and fry the onions till they turn translucent.
3. Add the shahjeera and fry for a few seconds. Add the tomato, green chillies and chilli powder and cook till the mixture leaves oil.
4. Add the cooked dal, coriander and paneer and cook for some time. Serve hot.

Snacks

ALOO PANEER CHAAT

   ⊷ Preparation time : 10 minutes.   ⊷ Cooking time : 15 minutes.   ⊷ Serves 4.

3 cups paneer (cottage cheese)
2 cups baby potatoes, boiled
2 cups green peas, boiled
25 mm. (1") piece ginger
5 to 6 green chillies, finely chopped
2 tbsp chaat masala
juice of 1 lemon
5 to 6 tbsp oil
salt to taste

For the garnish
¼ cup chopped coriander

1. Cut the paneer into 12 mm. (½") cubes.
2. Fry the paneer cubes and potatoes on a tava (griddle), adding a little oil at a time, till slightly brown in colour.

3. Remove and drain on absorbent paper. Keep aside.
4. Heat 2 tbsp of oil on the tava (griddle).
5. Add the peas and ginger and cook again for a while.
6. Add the potatoes, green chillies, chaat masala, lemon juice and salt. Serve hot, garnished with chopped coriander.

PANEER CHILLI CIGARS

Picture on facing page

◆ Preparation time : 5 minutes.   ◆ Cooking time : 10 minutes.   ◆ Makes 10 cigars.

5 samosa patti
1 tablespoon plain flour (maida) mixed with 1 tablespoon water

To be mixed into a fillling
¾ cup paneer (cottage cheese), crumbled
¼ cup spring onions, chopped
1 tbsp chilli-garlic sauce
¼ cup mozzarella cheese, grated
2 tsps oil
salt to taste

For the filling
1. Heat oil in a pan and sauté the spring onions till they are translucent.

Paneer Chilli Cigars : Recipe above →

2. Add all the remaining ingredients including the salt and mix well.
3. Cook for about 2 minutes and then divide into 10 equal portions. Keep aside.

How to proceed
1. Cut each samosa patti into 2 to get 125 mm. x 75 mm. (5" x 3") rectangular pieces. You will get 10 pieces in all.
2. Mix the flour and water to make flour paste. Keep aside.
3. Place a portion of the filling at one corner of the samosa patti piece. Roll it up tightly starting from the end where the filling is placed to make a cigar.
4. Seal the edge of the samosa patti piece using a little of the flour paste.
5. Repeat for the remaining pattis and filling.
6. Deep fry the cigars in hot oil till golden brown. Drain on absorbent paper. Serve hot with hot garlic sauce.

SESAME PANEER WITH HOT AND SWEET DIP

◈ Preparation time : 20 minutes.　◈ Cooking time : 20 minutes.　◈ Serves. 4.

For the sesame paneer
2 cups paneer (cottage cheese), cut into 75 mm. x 12 mm. (3" x ½") strips
¼ cup cornflour
2 tbsp plain flour (maida)
½ tsp soya sauce
½ cup sesame seeds (til)
salt to taste
oil for deep frying

For the hot and sweet dip
¼ cup sugar
½ tsp chilli powder
1 tbsp lemon juice
1 tsp salt

For the hot and sweet dip
1. Place the sugar and ½ cup of water in a pan and bring to a boil.
2. Cook till the syrup is of a 2 string consistency.
3. Add the chilli powder, lemon juice and salt and mix well.
4. Leave aside to cool.

How to proceed
1. In a bowl, combine the cornflour, plain flour, soya sauce and salt with ¼ cup of water to make a smooth batter. Use a whisk to remove any lumps.
2. Dip the paneer pieces in the batter and coat with the sesame seeds and deep fry in hot oil till they are golden brown.
3. Remove, drain on absorbent paper and serve hot with the hot and sweet dip.

CHILLI PANEER

◆ Preparation time : 10 minutes. ◆ Cooking time : 30 minutes. ◆ Serves 4.

¾ cup paneer (cottage cheese), cut into 12 mm. (½") thick strips
1 tsp grated ginger
2 tsp chopped garlic
2 tsp chopped celery
¼ cup spring onion whites, chopped
2 to 3 green chillies, cut into 25 mm. (1") pieces
¼ cup capsicum, sliced
1 tsp soya sauce
1 tsp sugar
1 tbsp cornflour mixed with 3 tbsp water
1 tsp oil
salt to taste

For the batter
¼ cup cornflour
¼ cup plain flour (maida)

59

1 tsp soya sauce
a pinch baking powder
salt to taste

Other ingredients
oil for deep frying

For the garnish
½ cup spring onion greens, chopped

1. Combine all the ingredients for the batter in a bowl and make a smooth batter by adding approx. ¼ cup of water. If there are lumps, use a whisk to remove them.
2. Coat the paneer pieces with the batter and deep fry in hot oil over a high flame till the paneer is golden brown.
3. Remove, drain on absorbent paper and keep aside.
4. Heat the oil in a pan and add the ginger, garlic, celery, spring onion whites and green chillies and sauté over a high flame for 1 to 2 minutes.
5. Add the capsicum and sauté for a few more seconds.
6. Add the soya sauce, sugar, cornflour paste and salt and allow it to come to a boil.
7. Toss in the fried paneer and mix well.
   Serve immediately, garnished with the spring onion greens.

CHEESY STUFFED POTATOES

❧ Preparation time : 5 minutes. ❧ Cooking time : 10 minutes. ❧ Serves 4.
❧ Baking time : 10 minutes. ❧ Baking temperature : 200°F (400°F).

4 large potatoes, boiled with the skin on
salt to taste

To be mixed into a filling
1 cup paneer (cottage cheese), grated
1 cup mozzarella cheese or cooking cheese, grated
3 green chillies, finely chopped
¼ cup celery, finely chopped
¼ tsp dried mixed herbs
salt to taste

1. Cut each potato horizontally into two halves.
2. Scoop a little of the centres of all the potato halves using a spoon so that a slight depression is formed for the filling.
3. Sprinkle the potato halves with salt and fill with the filling mixture.
4. Bake in a pre-heated oven at 200°C (400°F) for 4 to 5 minutes or until the cheese melts. Serve hot.

STUFFED SHAHI PURIS

❧ Preparation time : 15 minutes.   ❧ Cooking time : 20 minutes.   ❧ Makes 12 puris.

For the dough
2 cups fenugreek (methi) leaves, finely chopped
2 cups wheat flour (gehun ka atta) or plain flour (maida)
¼ tsp baking powder
1 tbsp fresh curds
2 tbsp melted ghee
salt to taste

To be mixed into a stuffing
1 cup paneer (cottage cheese), grated
2 tsp chopped green chillies
2 tbsp chopped coriander
salt to taste

Other ingredients
ghee or oil for deep frying

For the dough mixture
1. Sprinkle salt over the chopped fenugreek leaves and leave aside. After 15 minutes, squeeze out the water.
2. Mix the fenugreek leaves, flour, baking powder, curds and melted ghee and make a dough by adding a little water.
3. Divide the dough into 12 balls and roll out each ball into a small round. Keep aside.

How to proceed
1. Put 1 tsp of the stuffing in one round, fold the edges towards the centre and close. Roll out again.
2. Repeat for the remaining rounds and stuffing.
3. Deep fry in ghee. Remove, drain on absorbent paper and serve hot.

KAPI CHO PANEER

Picture on facing page

❧ Preparation time : 10 minutes. ❧ Cooking time : 10 minutes. ❧ Serves 4.

2 cups paneer (cottage cheese), cut into 12mm. (½") cubes
1 tsp chopped garlic
½ tsp chopped ginger
1 tsp chopped green chillies
1 tsp tomato ketchup
2 tbsp soya sauce
½ tsp chilli sauce
2 tsp cornflour mixed with ½ cup water
4 tbsp oil
salt to taste

For the garnish
½ cup spring onion greens, chopped

Kapi Cho Paneer : Recipe Above →

1. Heat the oil in a wok or frying pan on a high flame. Add the paneer cubes and cook on a high flame for a few minutes till the paneer is golden brown. Remove, drain on absorbent paper and keep aside.
2. In the same oil, add the garlic, ginger and green chillies and stir-fry for a few seconds. Add the paneer cubes, tomato ketchup, soya sauce, chilli sauce and salt and mix well.
3. Add the cornflour paste to the mixture and cook for 1 to 2 minutes.
   Serve hot garnished with the spring onion greens.

JHATPAT SAMOSA

❧ Preparation time : 3 minutes.   ❧ Cooking time : 10 minutes.   ❧ Makes 8 samosas.

8 samosas pattis

To be mixed into a filling
1 cup paneer (cottage cheese), grated
¾ cup onion, chopped
¼ cup capsicum, finely chopped
¼ tsp garam masala
1 tbsp lemon juice
salt to taste

Other ingredients
oil for deep frying

1. Place each samosa patti on a dry surface.
2. Put a teaspoonful of the filling in one corner of the samosa patti and roll into a triangle.
3. Seal the edges using a little water.
4. Deep fry in hot oil till golden brown. Remove, drain on absorbent paper. Serve hot.

LIFAFA PARATHAS

⚙ Preparation time : 15 minutes.   ⚙ Cooking time : 25 minutes.   ⚙ Makes 8.

For the parathas
2 cups plain flour (maida)
1 cup milk
1 tbsp melted ghee
1 tsp salt

For the filling
2 cups paneer, grated
1 cup chopped coriander
½ cup chopped mint (phudina) leaves
¼ cup onions, sliced
1 tsp lemon juice
1 tsp sugar
3 green chillies, chopped
salt to taste

Other ingredients
butter or ghee for cooking

For the parathas
1. Mix all the ingredients and make a soft, smooth dough adding water if required.
2. Divide into 8 equal portions and roll out small thin oblong parathas.
3. Cook on a tava (griddle) till brown spots appear. Keep aside.

For the filling
1. Combine the coriander, mint, onions, lemon juice, sugar, green chillies and salt with enough water and grind to a smooth paste to form a green chutney.
2. Mix together this chutney and paneer. Divide 8 portions and keep aside.

How to proceed
1. Put a portion of the stuffing in the centre of each paratha and close like an envelope.
2. Cook on a tava (griddle) on both sides with butter until golden brown.
3. Repeat for the remaining parathas and filling.
   Serve hot.

VARIATION : MINT PARATHAS
1. Instead of milk, you can prepare the dough using mint leaves water.
2. Mint leaves water can be made by blending mint leaves, water and a little lemon juice in a mixer.

PAPAD PANEER FRITTERS

⚜ Preparation time : 5 minutes. ⚜ Cooking time : 7 minutes. ⚜ Makes 6 pieces.

1 cup paneer (cottage cheese), cut into 25 mm.(1") cubes
2 tbsp red garlic chutney
2 papads, raw
¼ cup plain flour (maida)
salt to taste

Other ingredients
oil for deep frying

1. Slice each paneer cube into 2 halves. Keep aside.
2. Apply a little garlic chutney on ½ of the paneer cubes and sandwich with the remaining paneer cubes. Keep aside.
3. Grind the papads in a blender to a coarse powder. Keep aside.
4. Combine the flour with salt and ¼ cup of water to make a thin batter.
5. Coat the sandwiched paneer cubes with the flour batter and then roll them in powdered papad and keep aside.

6. Heat oil in a kadai and deep fry a few paneer pieces at a time, till golden brown in colour.
7. Remove, drain on absorbent paper and serve hot.

Handy tips : 1. Chilli-garlic sauce or Schezwan sauce can also be used instead of red garlic chutney.
2. Red garlic chutney is made by roasting garlic, dry red chillies and coconut in oil on a pan, adding tamarind pulp and salt to it and then grinding it.

PAHADI PANEER TIKAS

Picture on page 1

❧ Preparation time : 20 minutes. ❧ Cooking time : 15 minutes. ❧ Serves 6.

For the tikas
2 cups paneer (cottage cheese), cut into 25 mm. (1") cubes
1 cup onions, cut into 25 mm. (1") cubes
1 cup capsicums, cut into 25 mm. (1") cubes
2 cups tomatoes, cut into 25 mm. (1") cubes
1 tbsp fresh cream
2 tbsp fresh curds
1 tbsp oil
salt to taste

To be ground into a green marinade
1 cup mint leaves, chopped
½ cup coriander, chopped
1 tsp cumin seeds (jeera)
4 green chillies
1 tsp lemon juice

72

salt to taste

For the tikas
1. Apply half the green marinade on the paneer, onions, capsicum and tomatoes and arrange on skewers.
2. Cook on a barbeque for a few minutes. Alternatively, you could use the grill option of the oven or even use a tava (griddle).
3. When the edges turn golden brown, remove from the skewer and keep aside.

For the gravy
1. Heat the oil, add the remaining green marinade and fry for a while.
2. Add the cream, curds and salt and cook for some time. Keep side.

How to proceed
1. Arrange the tikas on a serving plate.
2. Pour the gravy immediately on top.
   Serve hot.

PANEER AND POTATO ROSTI

Picture on facing page

❧ Preparation time : 15 minutes.   ❧ Cooking time : 20 minutes.   ❧ Makes 4.

1 cup paneer (cottage cheese), grated
3 medium potatoes, par-boiled
½ cup onions, finely chopped
1 green chilli, finely chopped
½ cup processed cheese, grated
2 tbsp butter
salt and pepper to taste

1. Peel the potatoes. Grate coarsely. Sprinkle salt and pepper on top.
2. Melt the butter in a large frying pan. Add the onions and cook for 1 minute.
3. Add the green chilli, cheese and paneer and cook on a slow flame for a few
   seconds. Keep aside.
4. Add the potatoes and mix well.

Paneer and Potato Rosti : Recipe above ➔

5. Divide into 4 portions and keep aside.
6. Wet your fingers and spread each portion of the rosti on a hot greased non-stick pan to a circle of 6 mm. (¼") thickness.
7. Cook on both sides till golden brown.
   Serve hot.

Handy tips : 1. To parboil potatoes is to cook them till they are almost done but are still crunchy.
2. It is preferable to cook the potatoes over water and not in water when making rosti.

PANEER AND PEAS CHAAT

  Preparation time : 20 minutes.   Cooking time : 10 minutes.   Serves 6.

For the paneer cutlets
2 cups paneer (cottage cheese)
¼ cup coriander, chopped
2 green chillies, finely chopped
2 pinches sugar
¼ cup cornflour
cornflour for coating
oil for shallow frying
salt to taste

To be mixed together for the filling
1 tsp chopped cashewnuts
2 tsp chopped raisins (kishmis)

For the peas mixture
2 cups green peas or sprouted matki (moath beans), boiled
3 tbsp chopped coriander

2 green chillies, finely chopped
3 tbsp oil
salt to taste

To serve
beaten fresh curds
green chutney
khajur-imli ki chutney
papdi (puris used in chaat)
sev
chopped coriander

For the paneer cutlets
1. Mash the paneer thoroughly till smooth.
2. Add the coriander, green chillies, sugar, cornflour and salt and mix very well.
3. Divide into 20 equal portions and shape into small balls
4. Press the centre of each ball with your thumb, fill a little cashewnut- raisin mixture and bring the sides together to make tikkis.
5. Roll the tikkis in some cornflour.
6. Shallow fry in oil and keep aside.

For the peas mixture

Heat the oil in a pan and add the peas, coriander, green chilli and salt and fry for a few seconds. Keep aside.

How to serve

1. Place the hot paneer cutlets on a large serving plate, surround with the peas mixture and spread the curds, green chutney and khajur-imli ki chutney on top.
2. Arrange papdi on the border of the serving plate. Sprinkle sev and coriander on top and serve hot.
   Serve immediately.

Handy tip : Keep all the ingredients ready and assemble just before serving.

SPICY SUBMARINES

✤ Preparation time : 5 minutes.   ✤ Cooking time : 10 minutes.   ✤ Makes 4 submarines.

4 hot dog rolls

For the filling
½ cup paneer (cottage cheese), cut into 12 mm. (½") cubes
¼ cup spring onion whites, chopped
½ cup mushrooms, sliced
1 tsp Schezwan / chilli sauce
4 tbsp tomato ketchup
1 tbsp oil
salt to taste

Other ingredients
butter for cooking

For the garnish
grated paneer (cottage cheese)
spring onions greens

For the filling
1. Heat the oil in a saucepan, add all the ingredients and sauté for 2 minutes.
2. Divide into four portions and keep aside.

How to proceed
1. Slit each hot dog roll horizontally. Butter and toast lightly.
2. Stuff each hot dog roll with a portion of the filling.
   Garnish with the grated paneer and spring onion greens.

Handy tip : Schezwan sauce is readily available in bottles at most grocery stores.

STUFFED BAJRA ROTI

/ Preparation time : 10 minutes.   / Cooking time : 30 minutes.   / Makes 6 rotis.

For the dough
2 cups bajra flour (black millet flour)
a pinch salt

To be mixed into a stuffing
½ cup paneer (cottage cheese), crumbled
2 tbsp chopped fenugreek (methi) leaves
1 green chilli, finely chopped
1½ cups tomato, finely chopped
salt to taste

For the cooking
2 tbsp butter

1. For the dough, mix the bajra flour, salt and enough hot water to make a soft dough.
2. Knead well, divide into 12 equal portions and roll out each portion into thin rotis.

3. Spread a little stuffing on one roti. Then put another roti on top and press well so that it becomes one roti. Repeat for the remaining rotis and stuffing.
4. Cook each stuffed roti on a tava (griddle) on both sides with a little butter. Serve hot. If you like, apply a little butter before serving.

Handy tip : When making the dough using bajra flour, salt and hot water, start by mixing with a spoon and only then knead with your hands to prevent burning them.

PANEER WRAPS

Picture on facing page

❧ Preparation time : 25 minutes.　❧ Cooking time : 25 minutes.　❧ Makes 6.

For the wraps
1 cup wheat flour (gehun ka atta)
1 cup plain flour (maida)
4 tsp oil
½ tsp salt

For the stuffing
1 cup cauliflower, grated
1 cup paneer (cottage cheese), grated
3 chopped green chillies
2 tbsp chopped coriander
2 tsp oil
salt to taste

Other ingredients
oil for cooking

Paneer Wraps : Recipe above ➙

For the wraps
1. Mix the flours, oil and salt and make a smooth and pliable dough by adding enough warm water.
2. Knead the dough well and keep for ½ an hour. Knead again.
3. Divide into 6 portions and roll out each portion into 6" (150 mm) diameter rounds with the help of a little flour.
4. Cook lightly on both sides on a tava (griddle) using enough oil till they are well cooked.

For the stuffing
1. Heat the oil in a kadhai and add the green chillies and cauliflower.
2. Stir fry till the cauliflower is cooked.
3. Add the paneer, coriander and salt and cook for some time.
4. Divide into 6 portions and keep aside.

How to proceed
1. Place a hot wrap on a plate, place a portion of the stuffing on it.
2. Roll as shown in the picture and serve hot.

TANDOORI PANEER TIKAS

Picture on page 1

❧ Preparation Time : 20 minutes. ❧ Cooking Time : 15 minutes. ❧ Serves 6.

For the tikas
2 cups paneer (cottage cheese), cut into 25 mm. (1") cubes
1 cup onions, cut into 25 mm. (1") cubes
1 cup capsicum, cut into 25 mm. (1") cubes
1 cup tomatoes, pulp removed and cut into 25 mm. (1") cubes
1 tbsp oil

To be mixed into a tandoori marinade
¼ cup curds, beaten
1 tsp chilli powder
¼ tsp turmeric powder (haldi)
½ tsp ginger paste
¼ tsp garlic paste
¼ tsp Bengal gram flour (besan)
½ tsp chaat masala

½ tsp kasuri methi (dried fenugreek leaves)
½ tsp garam masala
2 drops red food colour (optional)
salt to taste

1. Marinate the paneer, onions, capsicum and tomato for about 20 minutes and then arrange on skewers.
2. Cook on barbeque for a few minutes. Alternatively, you could use the grill option of the oven or even just use a tava (griddle).
3. When the edges turn golden brown, remove from the skewer and serve hot with a chutney of your choice.

VARIATION : MAKHMALI PANEER

Picture on page 1

For the makhmali paneer
¼ cup curds
2 to 3 green chillies
25 mm. (1") piece ginger
5 to 6 cashewnuts
1 tsp mustard oil
salt to taste

1. Grind the green chillies, ginger and cashewnuts to smooth paste.
2. Whisk together this paste, curds, mustard oil and salt.
3. Substitute the tandoori marinade in the recipe above with this makhmali marinade to make makhmali paneer tikas.

CRISPY COTTAGE CHEESE TORTILLAS

* Preparation time : 25 minutes.   * Cooking time : 10 minutes.   * Serves 6.

For the corn tortilla
1 cup maize flour (makai ka atta)
¾ cup plain flour (maida)
3 tsp oil
¾ tsp salt
oil for deep frying

For the stuffing
2 cups paneer (cottage cheese), cut into small 12 mm. (½") cubes
1 tsp chopped green chilli
1 cup tomatoes, chopped
½ cup onion, chopped
¼ tsp oregano or thyme
2 tbsp oil
salt to taste

For the topping
fried capsicum strips

For the corn tortilla
1. Combine the flours, oil and salt and make a smooth dough by adding enough warm water.
2. Knead the dough well and keep aside for ½ hour. Knead again.
3. Roll out the tortilla dough into very small thin rounds (approx. 50 mm. (2") diameter).
4. Prick with a fork and deep fry in hot oil until crisp.
5. Remove drain on absorbent paper and store in an air-tight container.

For the stuffing
1. Heat the oil in a pan and sauté the onions for ½ minute.
2. Add the green chilli and tomatoes and fry again for ½ minute.
3. Add the paneer, oregano and salt and mix well.

How to proceed
1. Put some stuffing on each tortilla round and top with capsicum strips in a criss-cross.
2. Repeat with the remaining tortillas and stuffing.
   Serve hot.

ACHARI PANEER TIKAS

Picture on page 1

✥ Preparation time : 20 minutes.   ✥ Cooking time : 15 minutes.   ✥ Serves 4.

2 cups paneer (cottage cheese), cut into 25 mm. (1") cubes

For the achari marinade
¾ cup curds, hung
1 tbsp green chilli pickle
1 tsp chopped garlic
1 tsp fennel seeds (saunf)
½ tsp mustard seeds (rai)
¼ tsp fenugreek (methi) seeds
¼ tsp onion seeds (kalonji)
1 tsp cumin seeds (jeera)
¼ tsp turmeric powder (haldi)
1 tbsp mustard oil
salt to taste

1. Blend together the curds, green chilli pickle and garlic to a smooth paste.
2. Add the fennel seeds, mustard seeds, fennel seeds, cumin seeds, turmeric powder, mustard oil and salt and blend again so the spices are coarsely crushed.
3. Add the paneer and marinate for 20 minutes. Arrange on skewers.
4. Cook on a barbeque for a few minutes. Alternatively you could use the grill option of the oven or just use a tava (griddle).
5. When the edges turn golden brown, remove from the skewer and serve hot.

Handy tip : You can use any green chilli pickle of your choice.

CABBAGE AND PANEER ROLLS

❧ Preparation time : 15 minutes. ❧ Cooking time : 20 minutes. ❧ Makes 10 pieces.

10 fresh bread slices

For the stuffing
¾ cup paneer (cottage cheese), crumbled
1 cup cabbage, grated
2 tbsp chopped coriander
2 green chillies, finely chopped
salt to taste

Other ingredients
a few tbsp gram flour (besan) mixed with water
oil for frying

1. Cut and discard the bread crusts.
2. Roll out the slices using a rolling pin to flatten them. Keep aside.
3. Mix together the paneer, cabbage, paneer, coriander, green chillies and salt.

4. Divide the stuffing into 10 equal portions.
5. Place one portion of the stuffing in a corner of the bread slice and roll to form a cylinder.
6. Seal the edges with a paste made of equal quantity of gram flour and water.
7. Deep fry in hot oil until golden brown. Remove, drain on absorbent paper. Serve hot.

PANEER KHULCHAS

Preparation time : 15 minutes.   ‹§ Cooking time : 20 minutes.   ‹§ Makes 5 khulchas.

For the khulcha dough
1 cup plain flour (maida)
1 tsp (5 grams) fresh yeast, crumbled
1 tsp sugar
½ tsp salt
1 tbsp oil

For the paneer stuffing
½ cup paneer (cottage cheese), crumbled
1 green chilli, finely chopped
⅛ tsp turmeric powder (haldi)
¼ tsp kasuri methi (dried fenugreek leaves)
1 tsp oil
salt to taste

Other ingredients
oil for cooking

For the khulcha dough
1. Combine all the ingredients in a bowl and knead into a soft dough, using enough water until it is smooth and elastic (approx. 5 to 7 minutes).
2. Cover the dough with a wet muslin cloth and allow to prove till it doubles in volume (approx.15 to 20 minutes).
3. Press the dough lightly to remove the air.
4. Divide the dough into 5 equal portions. Keep aside.

For the paneer stuffing
1. Heat the oil in a pan, add the green chilli and fry for a few seconds.
2. Add the paneer, turmeric powder, kasuri methi and salt and mix well.
3. Allow to cool completely. Divide the stuffing into 5 equal portions and keep aside.

How to proceed
1. Roll out one portion of the khulcha dough into a 50 mm. (2") diameter circle.
2. Place one portion of the paneer stuffing in the centre of the circle.
3. Bring together all the sides in the centre and seal tightly.
4. Roll out again into a circle of 150 mm. (6") diameter, using flour to roll the khulcha.
5. Cook on a tava (griddle), using a little oil till both the sides are golden brown.

6. Repeat with the remaining dough and stuffing to make 4 more khulchas. Serve hot.

Handy tip : You can use ½ tsp of dried yeast dissolved in lukewarm water instead of fresh yeast for the above recipe.

⟶ SATAY STICKS ⟵

⚘ Preparation time : 10 minutes.   ⚘ Cooking time : 8 minutes.   ⚘ Serves 4.

½ cup paneer (cottage cheese), cut into 12 mm. (½") cubes
½ cup baby corn, cut into 25 mm. (1") pieces
½ cup green or red capsicum, cut into 12 mm. (½") cubes
1 tbsp oil

To be mixed into a marinade
2 tsp curry powder
2 tsp lemon juice
2 tsp honey
½ tsp salt
1 tbsp oil

For the peanut sauce
2 tbsp peanut butter
½ tsp soya sauce
1 tsp sugar

½ tsp chilli powder
salt to taste

For the peanut sauce
1. Combine all the ingredients in a pan with ½ cup of water. Mix well.
2. Bring the sauce to a boil. Remove and keep aside.

How to proceed
1. In a large bowl, combine the paneer, baby corn, capsicum and the prepared marinade and toss well.
2. Arrange a piece of paneer, capsicum and baby corn on a toothpick.
3. Repeat for the remaining vegetables (to make approximately 15 sticks).
4. Heat the oil on a tava (griddle) and sauté the satay sticks on all sides till the vegetables brown lightly (approximately 4 to 5 minutes). Serve hot with the peanut sauce.

PANEER TIKKA KATHI ROLLS

✺ Preparation time : 15 minutes.   ✺ Cooking time : 20 minutes.   ✺ Makes 9 rolls.

1 recipe tandoori paneer tikkas, page 87
2 cups plain flour (maida)
1 tbsp cornflour
½ tsp soda bicarb
½ tbsp butter
salt to taste

Other ingredients
oil for cooking

For the rotis
1. Sieve the flour, salt, cornflour and soda bicarb.
2. Rub in the butter and make a dough by adding enough milk or water.
3. Knead very well, cover and keep aside for ½ hour.
4. Knead once again and divide into 9 portions.
5. Roll each portion as thinly as possible. Cook lightly on a tava (griddle) and keep aside.
6. Divide the paneer tikka filling into 9 equal portions.
7. Spread one portion of the filling in the centre of each roti and roll up tightly.
8. When you want to serve, cook the rolls on a hot tava (griddle) using oil.
   Cut into 50 mm. (2") long pieces and serve hot.

Basic Recipe

~ TOMATO PURÉE ~

~ Preparation time : 2 minutes.   ~ Cooking time : 10 minutes.
~ Makes approx. 2 cups.

6 medium sized tomatoes

1. Bring to a boil a large vessel full of water.
2. Scoop out and discard the eyes of the tomatoes using the tip of the sharp knife.
3. Make a criss-cross cuts at the base of each tomato.
4. Put in boiling water for 3 to 4 minutes.
5. Remove and put in cold water for some time.
6. When the tomatoes are cool, peel and discard the skin.
7. Chop roughly and blend to a smooth purée in a blender.
   Use as required.

Handy tip : If frozen, tomato purée can last for months.

A magazine by **TARLA DALAL**

Book your copy now...

Price : Rs. 50/-

Available at your nearest bookstore, newspaper stands and tarladalal.com

SUBSCRIBE NOW & Get Free
Bonus Membership at tarladalal.com

Pick any one of the subscription offers and send us a cheque or a Demand Draft in favour of "Sanjay & Co." along with your detailed address including pin code, telephone no. and e-mail address.

Addressed to :

Sanjay & Co. 353, A-1, Shah & Nahar Industrial Estate, Dhanraj Mill Compound, Lower Parel (W), Mumbai 400013. INDIA

5 years (30 issues) + 1 Year Free Membership = Rs. 1450/-*

3 Years (18 issues) + 9 Months Free Membership = Rs. 1080/-*

1 Year (6 issues) + 2 Months Free Membership = Rs. 340/-*

*Offer valid for shipments only within India and is inclusive of shipping & handling charges.

For overseas shipments log on to tarladalal.com

For more information, call us on our helpline no. (022) 2496 8068 on all weekdays between 9.30 a.m. and 4.30 p.m. or write to us at subscription@tarladalal.com

Best sellers on INDIAN COOKING

by *Tarla Dalal*

Rotis & Subzis

Desi Khana

The Complete
Gujarati Cook Book